This edition copyright © 2002 Lion Publishing
Text copyright © 2002 Jean Watson

Published by
Lion Publishing plc
Mayfield House, 256 Banbury Road,
Oxford OX2 7DH, England
www.lion-publishing.co.uk
ISBN 0 7459 4645 3

First edition 2002
1 3 5 7 9 10 8 6 4 2 0

Acknowledgments

Scripture quotations are taken from the *Holy Bible, New International Version*,
copyright © 1973, 1978, 1984 by International Bible Society. Used by
permission.

75: The Lord's Prayer in its modern form, from *The Alternative Service Book 1980*,
copyright © The English Language Liturgical Consultation (ELLC) and
reproduced by permission of the publishers.

Every effort has been made to trace and acknowledge copyright holders of
all the quotations in this book. We apologize for any errors or omissions
that may remain, and would ask those concerned to contact the publishers,
who will ensure that full acknowledgment is made in the future.

Spelling and punctuation of quotations may have been modernized.

A catalogue record for this book is available
from the British Library

Typeset in 12/15 Venetian 301
Printed and bound in China

JEAN WATSON

All Through the Year

*A treasury of thoughts
to make each day special*

LION
Giftlines

January 1:
Life's Journey

Life is a journey of the heart that requires the mind. We must bring the truth into our hearts to guard and to guide our desire.

JOHN ELDREDGE

January 2:
Orientation

Where are you in your life's journey?

One way of arriving at an answer to this question might be to complete the following:

It is too late for…
It is too early for…
It is just right for…

Have a happy ending and a new beginning!

January 3:
Something New

All of us feel a little stuck or stale at times. Maybe all we need is rest. But sometimes it can help to do something completely different – take up a new interest or activity, for example, perhaps stepping out of our current interest and comfort zones.

January 4:
Loving Me, Loving You

Love your neighbour as yourself.

MARK 12:31

Loving myself isn't about indulging myself. It's about respecting and treating myself as a significant, valuable person. Treating others as significant, valuable people follows on from that.

January 5: Keeping Track

Have you ever considered keeping a journal? You don't have to write in it every day; just spare the time now and again to write down what's been happening and, more importantly, your thoughts and feelings about it. Such a journal can be a very good way of reflecting on your life, and of gaining perspective on it; making more sense of your unique story; and growing into your own unique identity.

January 6: The Heart of the Matter

Above all else, guard your heart, for it is the wellspring of life.

PROVERBS 4:23

Longing is the heart's treasury.

ST AUGUSTINE OF HIPPO

January 7: Rules for Life

Do to others as you would have them do to you.

LUKE 6:31

Robert Fulghum, philosopher, minister and writer, maintains that he learned all he really needed to know in kindergarten. Here are just a few of the things on his 'early learning' list:

share everything;
play fair;
clean up your own mess;
say sorry when you hurt somebody;
wash your hands before you eat;
be aware of wonder.

What would be on your list?

January 8:
Enchantment

I have heard it said that we lose the peace of years when we opt for the rapture of moments. We need wisdom to see the wrong kind of rapture coming, and willpower to take the right kind of action.

We are not free to choose by what we shall be enchanted, truly or falsely. In the case of a false enchantment, all we can do is to take immediate flight before the spell really takes hold.

W.H. AUDEN

January 9:
Going for Gold

Let us consider how we may spur one another on towards love and good deeds.

HEBREWS 10:24

January 10:
Friends

If I knew you and you knew me,
If both of us could clearly see,
And with an inner sight divine
The meaning of your heart
and mine,
I'm sure that we would differ less,
And clasp our hands in
friendliness;
Our thoughts would pleasantly
agree
If I knew you and you knew me.

NIXON WATERMAN

January 11:
Reality Check

Mental health is an ongoing process of dedication to reality at all costs.

M. SCOTT PECK

Week Two

January 12: Creativity

We do not need to be trained artists in order to show creativity. We can, if we want to, become more creative and imaginative in the way we send an e-mail, answer the phone, lay a table, greet callers or relate not just to friends but to the person at the supermarket checkout and others we encounter briefly in the course of our daily lives.

January 13: Stunning Theatre

What a different place the world would be if we all saw it as Calvin Seerveld does:

This world is the stunning theatre, workshop, playground of our Father in heaven, peopled by whatever his creative word sustains.

January 14: Walk with Beauty

Beauty is before me,
And beauty is behind me,
Above and below me hovers
  the beautiful,
I am surrounded by it,
I am immersed in it.

In my youth I am aware of it
And in my old age I shall walk
  quietly the beautiful trail.

NAVAHO BLESSING

January 15:
Ripples of Kindness

Do a deed of simple kindness;
Though its end you may not see,
It may reach, like widening
 ripples,
Down a long eternity.

JOSEPH NORRIS

January 16:
Surprised by Joy

*Into all our lives, in many simple,
familiar ways, God infuses joy
from the surprises of life: the success
we were not counting on; the blessing
we were not trying after; the strain
of music in the midst of drudgery;
the beautiful morning picture or sunset
glory thrown in as we pass to or from
our daily business; the unsought word
of encouragement or expression of
sympathy.*

SAMUEL LONGFELLOW

January 17:
Little by Little

There's a saying that goes:

*Life by the yard is hard,
but by the inch it's a cinch.*

I find that at times when life
feels overwhelming, it helps if
I focus on just one thing that
I can manage right now and
proceed on that basis, little by
little, one job at a time.

January 18:
What Price Assertion?

We are encouraged to be
assertive, but there are forms
of assertiveness that are very
like aggression. Assertiveness
should not be an expression of
ego but an expression of love.

Week Three

January 19:
Practising Peace

*Peace is not
something you wish for;
it's something you make,
something you do,
something you are, and
something you give away!*

ROBERT FULGHUM

January 20:
Criticism

I know someone whose stock response to criticism is: 'That's an awful thing to say!' He then proceeds to attack his critic's 'unkindness'. It seems to be his way of avoiding asking himself, 'Is what was said *true?*'

*He has the right to criticize
who has the heart to help.*

ABRAHAM LINCOLN

January 21:
Learning from Children

*The great man is he who
does not lose his child's heart.*

MENCIUS

*God sends children to enlarge our
hearts, and to make us unselfish
and full of kindly sympathies and
affections.*

MARY HOWITT

Make the most of the children you come into contact with.

January 22:
Not My Will

*Wounds from a friend
can be trusted.*

PROVERBS 27:6

I wanted joy: but thou didst
    know for me
That sorrow was the lift
    I needed most.

AUTHOR UNKNOWN

January 23:
The Rock Beneath

Nothing before, nothing
    behind;
The steps of faith
Fall on the seeming void,
    and find
The rock beneath.

JOHN GREENLEAF WHITTIER

January 24:
But Why?

My little granddaughter
has learned that when she says
'please' or 'very very careful' –
as in, 'I promise to be very
very careful' – she gets to eat
the biscuit, climb the stairs
or whatever. Usually. But when
these 'magic' words or phrases,
even pleadingly repeated, don't
'work', I find her bewilderment
and disappointment hard to
bear. I wonder whether God
feels like that when he too has
to deny our requests for reasons
beyond our understanding.

January 25:
Look Up

The sky is that beautiful
old parchment in which the sun
and the moon keep their diary.

ALFRED KREYMBORG

Look at the stars!
Look, look up at the skies!
O look at all the fire-folk
sitting in the air!

GERARD MANLEY HOPKINS

January 26:
Thank You

I thank you for the delights
of music and children, of other
men's thoughts and conversation
and their books to read by the fireside
or in bed with the rain falling on
the roof or the snow blowing past
outside the window.

LOUIS BROMFIELD

January 27:
Fresh Air

Mary was at the window in a
moment, and in a moment more
it was opened wide and freshness
and softness and scents and birds'
songs were pouring through.
'That's fresh air,' she said. 'Lie
on your back and draw in long
breaths of it.'

FRANCES HODGSON BURNETT

Is there enough fresh air in
your lungs and in your life?

January 28:
Helping

There may be times when you
cannot find help, but there is no
time when you cannot give help.

GEORGE S. MERRIAM

January 29:
Lone Rangers

You must give your burden to someone else, and you must carry someone else's burden. I'm sure that this is a law of the universe, and not to give up your parcel is as much to rebel as not to carry another's.

CHARLES WILLIAMS

January 30:
Do it Now

*S*o something needs to be done. Why not do it now? If you are inclined to procrastinate, follow that question with these:

If not now, when?
If not you, who?
If not here, where?
If not this way, what way?

January 31:
Doing Good…

*D*o all the good you can,
By all the means you can,
In all the ways you can,
In all the places you can.
At all the times you can,
To all the people you can,
As long as ever you can.

JOHN WESLEY

February 1:
… Thoughtfully!

*H*owever, in doing good we need to think long term as well as short.

If travellers on the Jerusalem to Jericho road were habitually beaten up and habitually cared for by good Samaritans, the need for better laws might well be overlooked.

PAUL TOURNIER

Week Five

February 2:
Good Behaviour

In the past children were brought up to consider questions such as, 'What kind of a world would it be, if everybody behaved like me?' A little heavy, perhaps, but very revealing!

February 3:
Leadership

A great leader never sets himself above his followers except in carrying responsibilities.

JULES ORMONT

Responsibility flourishes in a soil of reciprocal trust.

PETER BAELZ

Most of us have an area, however small, of which we are in charge. What kind of a leader are we being there?

February 4:
Doing Happy

If you observe a really happy man, you will find him building a boat, writing a symphony, educating his son, growing dahlias in his garden, or looking for dinosaur eggs in the Gobi desert. He will not be striving for it as a goal in itself.

W. BERAN WOLFE

I know that there is nothing better for men than to be happy and do good while they live.

ECCLESIASTES 3:12

Week Six

February 5:
Motivators

A sluggard does not plough in season; so at harvest time he looks but finds nothing.

PROVERBS 20:4

I have heard it said that the opposite of love isn't hate, it's laziness – the 'can't be bothered' attitude. It's certainly true that laziness frequently stems from lack of motivation, and the greatest motivator to action is love. Really loving people, it seems, *can* be bothered!

February 6:
Leisure Time

Only a man who can live with himself can enjoy the gift of leisure.

HENRY GREBER

February 7:
The Spice of Life

Human nature craves a certain amount of variety. We plant several kinds of flowers in our gardens. We enjoy our meals most when the selection of food is varied from day to day. The same principle applies to our daily activities.

HAROLD SHRYOCK

February 8:
The Risk of Beauty

When we return from happiness to our knowledge of life's misery, then beauty and art make us sad. But they remain beautiful. And the sorrow-steeped enchantment that rises from the miracle of beauty can endure for hours, for a lifetime.

HERMANN HESSE

February 9:
Smile!

*If we may believe our logicians,
man is distinguished from all other
creatures by the faculty of laughter.*

JOSEPH ADDISON

*Learn to laugh rather than be vexed
by other people's foibles, but learn the
ability also to let other people laugh
at your own.*

GERALD VANN

February 10:
Little Things

*Little books are read the most,
and little songs, the dearest loved.
And when Nature would make
anything especially rare and beautiful,
she makes it little: little pearls, little
diamonds, little dews. Life is made up
of little things that count.*

AUTHOR UNKNOWN

February 11:
Uniquely You

*If you have anything really
valuable to contribute to the world,
it will come through the expression
of your own personality.*

BRUCE BARTON

Given a secure and loving
environment, we develop our
own character and personality,
and this is expressed in
everything about us – the way
we live, relate, communicate;
our words, actions and reactions;
our beliefs and choices…
No one, absolutely no one else,
is a clone of you or me!

February 12:
Wonderful!

All things wise and wonderful,
The Lord God made them all.

CECIL FRANCES ALEXANDER

*Wonder is the opposite of cynicism
and boredom; it indicates that a person
has heightened aliveness, is interested,
expectant, responsive.*

ROLLO MAY

February 13:
Confidence

What is confidence? Not
to be confused with arrogance,
it comes, I suspect, from having
a sense of oneself as a separate,
worthwhile, effective and above
all loved person.

February 14:
Being Grown-Up

Robert Fulghum finds that
young people are usually longing
to be grown-up. So he gives them
a list of things that grown-ups
do, to sort out the men from the
boys — and the women from the
girls! It includes:

wipe runny noses;
clean up floor when the babies
    throw strained spinach;
empty the kitty box and scrape up
    the dog doo;
clean ovens and roasting pans.

February 15:
A Stitch in Time

*A man should keep his
friendships in constant repair.*

SAMUEL JOHNSON

Week Seven

February 16:
I Hear You...

I cannot hear a word you are saying, because what you are shouts so loudly in my ear.

AFRICAN PROVERB

Out of the overflow of the heart the mouth speaks.

MATTHEW 12:34

February 17:
Light a Candle

There's a lot wrong with the world. The news, if nothing else, rams that down our throats. So what should we do? Focus on the thousand-and-one things that are wrong and not know where to start… or change one thing for the better and start today?

February 18:
The Hound of Heaven

So long as we imagine that it is we who have to look for God, we must often lose heart. But it is the other way about; he is looking for us.

SIMON TUGWELL

I fled him, down the nights
　　and down the days,
Still with unhurrying chase,
And unperturbed pace,
Deliberate speed, majestic
　　instancy,
Came on the following feet.

FRANCIS THOMPSON

February 19:
The Home Stretch

*For now, our life is a journey
of high stakes and frequent danger.
But we have turned the corner; the
long years in exile are winding down
and we are approaching home.*

BRENT CURTIS AND JOHN ELDREDGE

February 20:
Only One

I am only one,
But still I am one.
I cannot do everything,
But still I can do something;
And because I cannot do
    everything
I will not refuse to do the
    something that I can do.

EDWARD EVERETT HALE

February 21:
Ways of Knowing

I have been thinking of the
different kinds of knowing that
we experience. Factual knowledge
is not the same as personal
knowledge. *Full* knowledge,
I believe, involves heart and head,
combining love and truth, caring
and wisdom. Whom do you know
in that complete, rounded way —
and vice versa?

February 22:
Where is God?

I sought to hear the voice
    of God
And climbed the topmost steeple,
But God declared, 'Go down
    again —
I dwell among the people.'

JOHN HENRY NEWMAN

Week Eight

February 23:
Happiness and Meaning

*Such happiness as life is
capable of comes from the full
participation of all our powers in
the endeavour to wrest from each
changing situation or experience
its own full and unique meaning.*

John Dewey

February 24:
World Unfinished

*God gave us a world unfinished,
so that we might share in the joys
and satisfactions of creation.*

Allen A. Stockdale

Can you give yourself time this
week to do something creative
for the environment, either with
others on a bigger scale or on
your own in your own garden
or window box?

February 25:
Plant a Tree?

I have some friends who
plant trees in local parkland
to celebrate special anniversaries
in their lives. I think this is a
wonderful, generous idea.

What does he plant who plants
    a tree?
He plants the friend of sun
    and sky;
He plants the flag of breezes free;
The shaft of beauty towering high.

Henry C. Bunne

February 26:
Love's Ingenuity

He drew a circle that shut me
out —
Heretic, rebel, a thing to flout.
But Love and I had the wit to win;
We drew a circle that took him in!

EDWIN MARKHAM

I am always moved by this verse.
It challenges me to think of ways
of including people.

February 27:
Going Deeper

*Superficiality is the curse of our age.
The desperate need today is not for a
greater number of intelligent people,
or gifted people, but for deep people.*

RICHARD FOSTER

February 28:
Is it Right?

*No man has any right to claim
a right, to indulge in a pleasure,
to demand a liberty which may be
the ruination of someone else.*

WILLIAM BARCLAY

*If people concentrated on their
responsibilities, others would have
their rights.*

STUART BRISCOE

We hear so much about rights
today… and so little about how
my rights affect others, and what
they require from others!

March 1:
This Day

I weave into my life today
The presence of God upon
my way.

DAVID ADAM

March 2:
Light in a Dark Place

*Those who sow in tears
will reap with songs of joy.*

PSALM 126:5

*Blessed are those who mourn,
for they will be comforted.*

MATTHEW 5:4

Let the hope in these verses
encourage you to play your –
perhaps painful – part in moving,
or helping someone else to move,
through tears to joy; through
grief to comfort.

March 3:
God Helps Those…

*I read of a man who had the
following sayings, among others,
up on the wall of his office:*

*'Always trust God. And always
build your house on high ground.'*

*'Always love thy neighbour. And
always pick a good neighbourhood
to live in.'*

ROBERT FULGHUM

March 4:
How Free is Free?

*Freedom means much more than
the opportunity to do what we like
or go where we want. A lot of people
do what they like but seldom like
what they do. Some have all the goods
of life, it seems, but no life. They have
everything to live with but nothing
to live for.*

FRANK POLLARD

March 5:
Successive Seasons

Quite apart from the delightful
varieties of beauty they offer to
my senses, the regularly recurring
seasons — with their familiar
webs, patterns and cycles —
reassure and soothe me.

I can but trust that good
  shall fall
At last — far off — at last, to all,
And every winter change to spring.

ALFRED, LORD TENNYSON

March 6:
New Life

*Death is unclasping; joy breaking
out in the desert; the heart come to its
blossoming time! Do we call it dying
when the bud bursts into flower?*

HENRY WARD BEECHER

March 7:
Spring

Nothing is so beautiful as
  Spring
When weeds, in wheels, shoot
  long and lovely and lush.

GERARD MANLEY HOPKINS

*The dewdrops on every blade of
grass are so much like silver drops
that I am obliged to stoop down as
I walk to see if they are pearls — and
those sprinkled on the ivy-woven beds
of primroses underneath the hazels,
whitethorns and maples are so like
gold beads that I stooped down to feel
if they were hard, but they melted
from my finger.*

JOHN CLARE

Find ways of letting spring's
whispers of hope touch you.

March 8:
Day by Day

We ought to hear at least one little song every day, read a good poem, see a first-rate painting, and if possible speak a few sensible words.

JOHANN WOLFGANG VON GOETHE

March 9:
The Future's Bright

Surely goodness and love will follow me all the days of my life.

PSALM 23:6

God had been in the past. Then he would be in the future too. Out in my future must lie more goodness, more mercy, more adventures, more friends.

CATHERINE MARSHALL

March 10:
Eye of the Beholder

What one approves, another scorns,
And thus his nature each discloses;
You find the rosebush full of thorns,
I find the thornbush full of roses.

ARTHUR GUITERMAN

March 11:
Here I Am

A German widow who hid some Jewish refugees in her home when the Nazis were in power was asked why she risked her life in this way. She replied, 'Because the time is now, and I am here.'

March 12:
A Single Whole

You have to be good to be wise;
for goodness and wisdom are two
aspects of a single whole.

DEREK KIDNER

March 13:
To Be a Pilgrim

Give me my scallop shell of
    quiet,
My staff of faith to walk upon,
My scrip of joy, immortal diet,
My bottle of salvation,
My gown of glory, hope's true
    gauge,
And thus I'll take my pilgrimage.

WALTER RALEIGH

March 14:
Projection

One thing I have learned
about others and myself is
that we often project on to
others what we see and dislike
in ourselves. Sometimes it
helps to realize that someone
who is making critical 'you are'
statements about me is really
trying to avoid making similar
'I am' statements about himself!

March 15:
Building Barriers?

People are lonely because
they build walls instead of bridges.

JOSEPH FORT NEWTON

On the other hand:

Good fences make good neighbours.

ROBERT FROST

March 16:
Heaven

In heaven we will live more fully and satisfyingly than ever before. And that life will involve all the really important elements of what we know as life: relationships, development, knowledge, communication.

DAVID WINTER

I would only want to add one thing: creativity.

March 17:
Live the Moment

One of the most tragic things I know about human nature is that all of us tend to put off living. We are all dreaming of some magical rose garden over the horizon — instead of enjoying the roses that are blooming outside the windows today.

DALE CARNEGIE

March 18:
The Gift of Space

We can offer a space where people are encouraged to disarm themselves, to lay aside their occupations and preoccupations and to listen with attention and care to the voices speaking in their own centre.

HENRI NOUWEN

Could you offer this kind of space to one person this coming week? Or maybe find it for yourself?

March 19:
Sobering Thought?

It's hard to believe the world is here just so I can party, when a third of its people go to bed starving each night.

Philip Yancey

March 20:
A Kind of Dying

God does not die on the day when we cease to believe in a personal deity, but we die on the day when our lives cease to be illumined by the steady radiance, renewed daily, of a wonder, the source of which is beyond all reason.

Dag Hammarskjöld

March 21:
Paying Attention

It is so easy to rush through life without paying enough attention to what really matters: the people we love and are loved by, and the fascination and beauty of our surroundings. I know that I need to give myself time to use both my physical senses and my inward ones: the eyes and ears of my heart, mind and imagination.

March 22:
There Must Be More

The notion that what we happen to apprehend directly with our five senses is all the reality there is now seems to me to be almost grotesquely parochial. And this conviction is the bedrock of whatever religious faith I have: there must be more than this.

Philip Toynbee

Week Twelve

March 23:
Dig for Loveliness

*Whatever is true, whatever is
noble, whatever is right, whatever is
pure, whatever is lovely, whatever
is admirable — if anything is
excellent or praiseworthy — think
about such things.*

<small>PHILIPPIANS 4:8</small>

We might have to dig to uncover
excellence — wonderful things,
admirable people — in our world,
but the effort is worth it: it's
such a tonic, in the midst of all
the bad news that is thrust at us,
to take in some of the good news.

March 24:
Love's Welcome

*Love bade me welcome;
    yet my soul drew back,
Guilty of dust and sin.
But quick-eyed Love,
    observing me grow slack
From my first entrance in,
Drew nearer to me,
    sweetly questioning
If I lacked anything.*

<small>GEORGE HERBERT</small>

March 25:
Earth's Soul

*The shape of the landscape
is an ancient and silent form of
consciousness. Mountains are
huge contemplatives. Rivers and
streams offer voice; they are the
tears of the earth's joy and despair.
The earth is full of soul.*

<small>JOHN O'DONOHUE</small>

March 26:
Problems for Growth

When we desire to encourage
the growth of the human spirit, we
challenge and encourage the human
capacity to solve problems, just as
we deliberately set problems for our
children to solve. It is through the
pain of confronting and resolving
problems that we learn.

M. SCOTT PECK

March 27:
Divine Alchemy

If we see God everywhere,
in each event, either intentionally
or permissively but always creatively,
then we can take heart and be assured
that our trouble is not totally bad or
beyond the possibility of working good.

JOHN R. CLAYPOOL

March 28:
Word Watch

Blessed is the one who, having
nothing to say, abstains from giving
in words evidence of the fact.

GEORGE ELIOT

The tongue is a small part of the body,
but it makes great boasts. Consider
what a great forest is set on fire by
a small spark.

JAMES 3:5

If I speak in the tongues of men and
of angels, but have not love, I am only
a resounding gong or a clanging
cymbal.

1 CORINTHIANS 13:1

March 29:
To Err is Human

More and more, I think we need to have as our stated or unstated bottom line, 'I could be wrong.' Without it, real dialogue is impossible. Strong opinions and passionate beliefs *can* be held in conjunction with an awareness of what we don't know, so that we remain humble and open, ready to listen to others and rethink if necessary.

March 30:
Normality

Religious experience is normal experience understood at full depth.

Professor Jeffreys

March 31:
Priorities

I learned not to let the urgent get in the way of the important. The urgent is the paperwork on my desk, my appointments, my daily routine. The important is my faith, my family, my friends and my relationships.

Kay You

O Lord, help me to put first things first and second things second.

April 1:
Treasures of Life

If you had to choose five words to describe life's deepest treasures, what would they be? I think mine would begin with LOVE, JOY, PEACE, and end with FAITH and HOPE.

Week Fourteen

April 2:
Treasures of Pain

*Stars may be seen from the bottom
of a deep well when they cannot be
discerned from the top of a mountain:
so are many things learned in adversity
which the prosperous dream not of.*

C.H. SPURGEON

April 3:
Neighbours

*'To whom am I a neighbour?'
means, 'Where is someone who
needs my help?*

HEINZ VONHOFF

Of course, the same applies
when the boot is on the other
foot: 'I need help – where is
my neighbour?'

April 4:
Creative Tension

Conflict can be intimidating.
And yet, when we become so
afraid of it that we even try to
avoid creative tension, debate,
questioning and the good kinds
of confrontation, we run the
risk of missing out at the same
time on certain very necessary
life skills: listening to other
people's opinions, developing
and expressing our own ideas;
discussing and resolving issues,
differences, misunderstandings…

April 5:
The Stronger Things

*Life is stronger than death,
light stronger than darkness
and love stronger than hate.*

JEAN VANIER

April 6:
Grandfather in Heaven?

We want not so much a Father in heaven as a grandfather in heaven, whose plan for the universe was such that it might be said at the end of each day, 'A good time was had by all.' I should very much like to live in a universe which was governed on such lines but, since it is abundantly clear that I don't and since I have reason to believe nevertheless that God is love, I conclude my perception of love needs correction.

C.S. LEWIS

April 7:
Just Two Things

Freedom and a country where he could live in safety: David wanted both. 'But nothing more,' he told himself. 'Just those two things and that will be enough. Johannes said greedy people can never be happy, and I would so much like to know what it feels like to be happy.'

ANNE HOLM

April 8:
Friendship

I have a few very close and confidential friends. We talk. We think. We evaluate decisions. We share our struggles. We pray. We are available and we are in touch. Our goal is to strengthen and help one another in any way we can.

CHARLES R. SWINDOLL

Week Fifteen

April 9:
Green Hope

*The greening of the trees is an
eloquent allegorical expression of
some of the claims that Easter makes:
that nothing is hopeless; that creation
is forgiving and resourceful; that the
worst of us, the worst of times, is
constantly given a new chance.*

JOHN WHALE

April 11:
The Miracle of Spring

*If spring came but once a century
instead of once a year, or burst forth
with the sound of an earthquake and
not in silence, what wonder and
expectation there would be in all hearts
to behold the miraculous change.*

HENRY WADSWORTH LONGFELLOW

April 10:
Recovery

Who would have thought my
shrivelled heart
Could have recovered greenness?

GEORGE HERBERT

April 12:
Small Pleasures

I love the small pleasures of life.
If the doors are too low, I bend;
If I can remove a stone from
the path I do so;
If it is too heavy, I go round it.
I find something in every day
that pleases me.

GOETHE'S MOTHER

Week Fifteen

April 13:
Forgiveness

I know someone who doesn't believe in forgiveness. So he carries an increasingly heavy burden of guilt and unfinished business around with him.

Who is a God like you,
who pardons sin?

MICAH 7:18

April 14:
All in the April Evening

All in the April evening,
April airs were abroad;
I saw the sheep with their lambs,
And thought on the Lamb of God.

KATHERINE TYNAN

April 15:
Easter Saturday

Just as Good Friday demolished the instinctive belief that this life is supposed to be fair, Easter Sunday followed with its startling clue to the riddle of the universe. Out of the darkness a bright light shone.
The Cross of Christ may have overcome evil, but it did not overcome unfairness. For that, Easter is required. Meanwhile we live out our days on Easter Saturday.

PHILIP YANCEY

Week Sixteen

April 16:
SuperGod?

I think it depends on your image of God, whether you see God as a superman who swoops down and intervenes; but I think God sometimes asks you to be feet and hands to your own prayers.

SYLVIA SANDS

April 17:
Imagination

For the alert and wakened imagination, possibilities always beckon towards new pathways of creativity, belonging and love. Each of us has been created by the Divine Artist, made in the image and likeness of the Divine Imagination.

JOHN O'DONOHUE

April 18:
Seize the Moment

Three things return not, even
  for prayers and tears –
The arrow which the archer
  shoots at will;
The spoken word, keen-edged
  and sharp to sting;
The opportunity left unimproved.
If thou would'st speak a word of
  loving cheer,
O, speak it now. The moment is
  thine own.

AUTHOR UNKNOWN

April 19:
Taking Root

We must go out and re-ally ourselves to Nature every day. We must take root, send out some little fibre at least, even every winter day. I am sensible that I am imbibing health when I open my mouth to the wind.

HENRY DAVID THOREAU

April 20:
Interdependence

A hundred times every day I remind myself that my inner and my outer life depend on the labours of other men, living and dead, and that I must exert myself in order to give in some measure as I have received and am still receiving.

ALBERT EINSTEIN

April 21:
Moved by Kindness

Set a high value on spontaneous kindness.

SAMUEL JOHNSON

Is it true for you, as it is for me, that when we are stressed and sad, it is people's kindness that really moves, touches and inspires us?

April 22:
Light Relief

From troubles of the world, I turn to ducks, Beautiful, comical things…

F.W. HARVEY

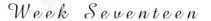

April 23:
True Meaning

*Our role in the world that
is given us is to wonder at it,
to explore it, and to restore to it
and to our lives their true meaning.
We were intended to receive creation
as we receive our lives, thankfully
as a gift.*

MICHAEL MAYNE

April 24:
Being Responsible

*Liberty means responsibility.
That is why most men dread it.*

GEORGE BERNARD SHAW

*You become responsible, for ever,
for what you have tamed.*

ANTOINE DE SAINT-EXUPÉRY

April 25:
Marks of Maturity

*I have learned to be content
whatever the circumstances.*

PHILIPPIANS 4:11

It has been said that mature
people are able to affirm others
and to be flexible; they are
confident in that they have a
secure sense of who they are;
and they are contented in that
they make the most of who they
are and what they have, while
being realistic about and
accepting their limitations.

April 26:
Me First!

Ours is a day of self-promotion, defending our own rights, taking care of ourselves first, winning by intimidation, pushing for first place, and a dozen other self-serving agendas. That one attitude does more to squelch our joy than any other.

CHARLES R. SWINDOLL

April 27:
Unworthy Motives

I was very struck once by something someone said to me with regard to decision-making. It happened a long time ago, but I've never forgotten it. She said, 'My fiancé and I agreed that if ever money were the only reason for doing something, it would be a no-no.'

April 28:
Healthy Laughter

Virtually every day I can find at least one thing to laugh about. Experts tell us that laughter not only makes our serious lives lighter, but also helps control pain.

CHARLES R. SWINDOLL

Laughter is a tranquillizer with no side effects.

ARNOLD GLASOW

April 29:
Perfectionism

Perfectionists have dreadful trouble trying to live in this imperfect world with imperfect people!

April 30:
Diversity

Every single one of us is unique. Of course there are similarities, but you and I are not exactly like any of the other six billion or so people ever born into this world. This makes me want to resist the kind of standardizing and uniformity that cuts out individual creativity and originality for the sake of profit or neatness.

May 1:
Intricate Interaction

Every single interaction of every single particle has to lock into place with every other with a precise and intricate delicacy in order to produce exactly this universe.

ANGELA TILBY

May 2:
Unafraid to Hope

Do not fear to hope…
Each time we smell the autumn's
    dying scent,
We know that primrose time will
    come again.

SAMUEL TAYLOR COLERIDGE

Fear of being disappointed can make us afraid to hope. But without hope life is flat and empty. Besides, look around, and you will find grounds for and parables of hope everywhere.

May 3:
Ways of Being

Cultivate freedom of spirit, spaciousness of mind: live in peace, boldly and with tranquillity.

ABBÉ DE TOURVILLE

May 4:
Listening

*Listen to me for a day —
an hour — a moment, lest
I expire in my terrible
wilderness, my lonely silence.*

SENECA

Nothing has changed since
Seneca's day in this respect.
People, many people, are still
desperate for those who will
truly listen to them — their
stories, their deep secret selves.
Could you be someone's lifeline
today? Or could someone else
be yours?

May 5:
Happy Places

*Sometimes since I've been in
the garden I've looked up through
the trees at the sky and I have had
a strange feeling of being happy,
as if something were pushing and
drawing in my chest and making
me breathe fast.*

FRANCES HODGSON BURNETT

Where are your happy places, and
how often do you go to them?

May 6:
Not Just a Dream

*Hoping is not dreaming. It is
not spinning an illusion of fantasy
to protect us from our boredom or
our pain. It means a confident alert
expectation that God will do what
he said he will do. It is imagination
put in the harness of faith.*

EUGENE PETERSON

Week Nineteen

May 7:
This New Day

*This is the day the Lord
has made; let us rejoice and
be glad in it.*

PSALM 118:24

May 8:
One Mouth, Two Ears

It has often been said that
we have one mouth and two
ears so as to say less and listen
more. This is certainly something
I subscribe to; whether I always
manage to do it is another matter!
But courses in listening and,
more particularly, my experience
of loss have made me far more
aware of the value of genuine
listening offered to and by
others.

May 9:
Facing Ourselves

How well do you know
yourself? Sometimes it is our
reactions to others that alert us
to ourselves. When we come
down very hard on someone
else, it's often because they are
displaying faults we know we
have. Facing up to these and
other aspects of ourselves may
be hard. But as we understand
ourselves better, we can become
more consistent and whole and
grow in our ability to relate
well to others.

Week Nineteen

May 10:
Sensation

God is not far away from us, altogether apart from the world we see, touch, hear, smell and taste about us. Rather, he awaits us every instant in our action, in the work of the moment. He is at the tip of my pen, my brush, my needle – of my heart and of my thought.

PIERRE TEILHARD DE CHARDIN

May 11:
A Different Drummer

If a man does not keep pace with his companions, perhaps it is because he hears a different drummer. Let him step to the music he hears, however measured or far away.

HENRY DAVID THOREAU

May 12:
Good Work

O to your birthright and
   yourselves,
To your own souls be true!
A weary, wretched life is theirs,
Who have no work to do.

ORME

May 13:
I Forgive You

Everyone says forgiveness is a lovely idea, until they have something to forgive.

C.S. LEWIS

He who cannot forgive breaks the bridge over which he must pass himself.

GEORGE HERBERT

May 14:
Security

When you pass through the waters, I will be with you; and when you pass through the rivers, they will not sweep over you.

ISAIAH 43:2

When trouble hits us we can let it knock us out, so that we lose all hope and stamina. Or we can accept it without defeat, rebellion or evasion, trusting that God will make clear tomorrow what is so difficult to understand today.

GEORGE APPLETON

May 15:
Heaven and Earth

Earth's crammed with heaven, And every common bush afire with God.

ELIZABETH BARRETT BROWNING

May 16:
Humility

Have you heard of the woman who said, 'I pride myself on my humility'? Humility isn't a way of concealing pride or manipulating others to do what we want; and it's not about being a doormat or feeling worthless. It's an attitude and a choice springing from love and a desire to help and care for others.

May 17:
In Memoriam

I hold it true, whate'er befall; I feel it, when I sorrow most; 'Tis better to have loved and lost Than never to have loved at all.

ALFRED, LORD TENNYSON

Week Twenty

May 18:
No Man is an Island

Simon and Garfunkel sang, 'I am a rock, I am an island… for a rock feels no pain and an island never cries.' If you don't or can't laugh, cry, feel joy, feel pain, perhaps you need healing love. Do you *want* it?

May 19:
Travelling Hopefully

To travel hopefully is a better thing than to arrive, and the true success is to labour.

ROBERT LOUIS STEVENSON

The little dissatisfaction which every artist feels at the completion of a work forms the germ of a new work.

AUTHOR UNKNOWN

May 20:
On the Line

Every day I put faith on the line. I have never seen God. In a world where nearly everything can be weighed, explained, quantified, subjected to psychological analysis and scientific control, I persist in making the centre of my life a God whom no eye hath seen, nor ear heard, whose will no one can probe. That's a risk.

EUGENE PETERSON

May 21:
Right and Wrong

If I am right, thy grace impart,
Still in the right to stay;
If I am wrong, O teach my heart
To find the better way.

ALEXANDER POPE

May 22:
Hospitality

*Our society seems to be increasingly
full of fearful, defensive, aggressive
people anxiously clinging to their
property and inclined to look at their
surrounding world with suspicion,
always expecting an enemy to suddenly
appear, intrude and do harm. Our
vocation is to convert the enemy into a
guest and to create the free and fearless
space where brotherhood and sisterhood
can be formed and fully experienced.*

HENRI NOUWEN

May 23:
Not Necessarily!

I have been thinking that bigger,
faster, easier is not necessarily
better. As people rightly point
out, 'Small is beautiful,' 'There's
more to life than increasing its
speed,' 'Effort develops muscle
and stamina.' For example, I need
and value my car very much, but
if it means that I never walk
anywhere, a whole range of
human contacts and exchanges
that could occur, don't. Quite
apart from the health benefits
of walking, or the chance it gives
me to stop and smell the roses!

May 24:
First Things First

*The great use of life is to spend it
for something that outlasts it.*

WILLIAM JAMES

Week Twenty-One

May 25:
No Closer Friend

'Eternity' is there,
We say, as of a Station.
Meanwhile he is so near,
He joins me in my Ramble –
Divides abode with me –
No Friend have I that so persists
As this Eternity.

EMILY DICKINSON

May 26:
Feeling Good

Laughter is the sensation of
feeling good all over and showing it
principally in one place.

JOSH BILLINGS

The cheerful heart has a
continual feast.

PROVERBS 15:15

May 27:
Get Better!

We are often urged, 'Don't get mad, get even.' But any short-term feelings of satisfaction we may gain by doing that aren't worth it. We can do better than getting even. We can refuse to behave badly, and instead gain perspective and control.

Do not take revenge, my friends,
for it is written: 'It is mine to avenge;
I will repay.' On the contrary:
'If your enemy is hungry, feed him.'

ROMANS 12:19–20

May 28:
Step into Joy

My soul is heavy with sunshine
and steeped with strength.
The sunbeams have filled me like
a honeycomb,
It is the moment of fullness,
And the top of the morning.

D.H. LAWRENCE

May 29:
A Forgotten Blaze

At the back of our brains,
so to speak, there is a forgotten
blaze or burst of astonishment
at our own existence. The object
of the artistic and spiritual life is
to dig for this sunrise of wonder.

G.K. CHESTERTON

May 30:
Perfect Healing?

Some would have us believe
that we can be perfectly healed
and whole now. I don't believe it.
We can experience relief, remission,
healing – whatever we choose to
call it. But I suspect that all of
us have to live with unhealed
bits of ourselves; with pain, with
contradictions and dilemmas.
The question is, will we let them
warp us or will we bring some
good and meaning out of even
these things?

May 31:
Compassion

Teach me to feel another's woe,
To hide the fault I see;
That mercy I to others show,
That mercy show to me.

ALEXANDER POPE

June 1: Nature's Beauties

Nature reaches out to us with welcoming arms, and bids us enjoy her beauty; but we dread her silence and rush into the crowded cities, there to huddle like sheep fleeing from a ferocious wolf.

KAHLIL GIBRAN

Go forth under the open sky and listen to Nature's teachings.

WILLIAM CULLEN BRYANT

June 2: Making a Difference

When we do the best we can, we never know what miracle is wrought in our life, or in the life of another.

HELEN KELLER

June 3: Four Sweet Months

First, April, she with mellow
    showers,
Opens the way for early flowers;
Then after her comes smiling May,
In a more rich and sweet array:
Next enters June, and brings us
    more
Gems than those two that went
    before:
Then (lastly) July comes, and she
More wealth brings in, than all
    those three.

ROBERT HERRICK

Week Twenty-Three

June 4:
Identity

Identity is found in living in
the midst of a constantly changing
inner and outer world and growing
in a sense of peace with oneself,
with God and with other people.

DICK KEYES

June 5:
Take Time

Take time to think –
It is the source of power.
Take time to read –
It is the fountain of wisdom.
Take time to be friendly –
It is the road to happiness.
Take time to give –
It is too short a day to be selfish.
Take time to pray –
It is the greatest power on earth.

AUTHOR UNKNOWN

June 6:
More and More

The more a soul loves,
the more it longs,
the more it hopes,
the more it finds.

JEAN-PIERRE DE CAUSSADE

June 7:
Refreshment

I felt as if I'd been a blocked
spring, and someone had cleaned me
so that the water could gush out
fresh and strong.

MARY RAY

After recovering from a near-
death experience, Admiral Byng
wrote:

I did take away something that
I had not fully appreciated before;
appreciation of the sheer beauty
and miracle of being alive.

Week Twenty-Three

June 8:
Presence

In the absence of any other proof,
the thumb alone would convince me
of God's existence.

ISAAC NEWTON

God never leaves identical fingerprints.

AUTHOR UNKNOWN

Beauty is God's handwriting.

CHARLES KINGSLEY

June 9:
Then and Now

The Past can be no more –
Whose misemploying I deplore:
The Future is to me
An absolute uncertainty:
The Now, which will not with me
* stay,*
Within a second flies away!

THOMAS KEN

June 10:
Giving and Gaining

What I kept I lost;
what I gave I have.

PERSIAN PROVERB

Whoever loves money
never has money enough.

ECCLESIASTES 5:10

Whereas material goods are
diminished by sharing, the spiritual
treasuries of knowledge and of beauty,
of poetry, music and the rest, by being
shared are not diminished but
increased.

KATHLEEN RAINE

June 11:
Art as Therapy

In his Nobel Prize lecture Aleksandr Solzhenitsyn said:

Art can thaw out even a frozen, darkened soul and bring it to a high spiritual experience.

Certainly the work that is being done with handicapped and disturbed children and in prisons would suggest that art can be therapeutic in all sorts of ways.

June 12:
A Lonely Place

Let us live our lives to the fullest, but let us not forget once in a while to get up long before dawn to leave the house and go to a lonely place.

HENRI NOUWEN

June 13:
The Way of Friendship

We cannot tell the precise moment when friendship is formed. As in filling a vessel drop by drop, there is at last a drop which makes it run over; so in a series of kindnesses there is at last one which makes the heart run over.

SAMUEL JOHNSON

No man is useless while he has a friend.

ROBERT LOUIS STEVENSON

June 14:
Rainbows

Walk on a rainbow trail;
walk on a trail of song,
and all about you will be beauty.
There is a way out
of every dark mist,
over a rainbow trail.

NAVAHO SONG

Week Twenty-Four

June 15:
Joy Blossoms

You cannot seek ecstatic moments directly; you must be surprised by joy.

ABRAHAM MASLOW

Just as a plant grows when the conditions – sunshine, soil, rain and tending – are right, so joy blossoms in the context of healthy, harmonious, productive lifestyles and relationships.

June 16:
Self-Expression

Anything is free when it spontaneously expresses its own nature to the full in activity.

JOHN MACMURRAY

Creativity is not merely permissible, it is essential. To express ourselves in art is to experience more fully the richness of being human.

STEVE TURNER

June 17:
Dreams

Hold fast to dreams
For if dreams die
Life is a broken-winged bird
That cannot fly.

LANGSTON HUGHES

We need our dreams. But any dream won't do. Only those that fit who we are will stretch and inspire us appropriately rather than frustrate, damage or even destroy us.

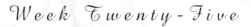
June 18:
Down But Not Out

*We are hard pressed on every
side, but not crushed; perplexed,
but not in despair; persecuted,
but not abandoned; struck down,
but not destroyed.*

2 Corinthians 4:8–9

June 19:
Friends Reunited

*Friendship, like a severed bone,
Improves, and gains a stronger
tone,
When aptly reunited.*

William Cowper

This is especially true, perhaps,
when the exchange of letters has
bridged the gap while friends
have been separated from one
another.

June 20:
Strain and Stress

*Drop thy still dews of quietness
Till all our strivings cease;
Take from our souls the strain
and stress
And let our ordered lives confess
The beauty of thy peace.*

John Greenleaf Whittier

June 21:
Heartfelt!

*The best and most beautiful
things in the world must be felt
with the heart.*

Helen Keller

Week Twenty-Five

June 22:
Count Your Blessings

If you woke up this morning with more health than illness, you are more blessed than the million who will not survive this week. If you have never experienced the danger of battle, the loneliness of imprisonment, the agony of torture, or the pangs of starvation, you are ahead of five hundred million people in the world.

AUTHOR UNKNOWN

June 23:
Heaven on Earth

Work like you don't need the
money,
Love like you've never been hurt,
Dance like nobody's watching,
Sing like nobody's listening,
Live like it's heaven on earth.

AUTHOR UNKNOWN

June 24:
Mouth Music

Take time to laugh:
It is the music of the mouth.

AUTHOR UNKNOWN

The Rector will preach his farewell message, after which the choir will sing, 'Break forth into joy.'

CHURCH NEWS CLIPPING

Little boy to his vicar:

I don't pray every night because there are some nights when I don't need anything.

Week Twenty-Six

June 25:
Statistics

If we could shrink the earth's population to 100 people with all the existing ratios as they are at the time of writing:
6 people would possess 59% of the world's wealth;
80 would live in substandard housing;
70 would be unable to read;
50 would suffer from malnutrition.

What can I do, however small, to bring about greater justice and equality?

June 26:
Practical Goodness

He who would do good must do it in minute particulars.

WILLIAM BLAKE

June 27:
Inner Struggle

When I want to do good, evil is right there with me.

ROMANS 7:21

Child to parent:

When you say 'must'
I feel 'won't' all over.

We can all identify with the above!

June 28:
Joy Everywhere

Joy is everywhere; it is in
the earth's green covering of grass;
in the blue serenity of the sky; in
the reckless exuberance of spring; in
the severe abstinence of grey winter;
in the living flesh that animates
our bodily frame; in the exercise
of all our powers.

RABINDRANATH TAGORE

Week Twenty-Six

June 29:
An Eye for Splendour

Most people simply don't know how beautiful the world is and how much splendour is revealed in the smallest things, in a common flower, in a stone, in the bark of a tree or the leaf of a birch. Grown-up people gradually lose the eye for these riches which children quickly notice and love with their whole heart.

RAINER MARIA RILKE

June 30:
Travelling

My dearest Lord,
Be thou a bright flame before me,
Be thou a guiding star above me,
Be thou a smooth path beneath me,
Be thou a kindly shepherd behind me,
Today and for evermore.

ST COLUMBA OF IONA

July 1:
Ways of Seeing

The spider holds a silver ball
In unperceived hands
And dancing softly to himself
His yarn of pearl unwinds.

EMILY DICKINSON

To see a world in a grain of sand,
And heaven in a wild flower:
Hold infinity in the palm of your
hand,
And eternity in an hour.

WILLIAM BLAKE

Week Twenty-Seven

July 2:
Good Times and Bad

It is easy for me to worship in the summer sunshine when the melodies of life are in the air and the fruits of life are on the tree. But let the song of the bird cease and the fruit of the tree fall, and will my heart still go on to sing?

GEORGE MATHESON

July 3:
A Second Mile

If someone forces you to go one mile, go with him two miles.

MATTHEW 5:41

Are you a 'second-mile' person? I have come across people like this in the most unexpected and unlikely places – and what a blessing they are!

July 4:
When One Door Closes

Enable us to see each temporarily closed door as your leading towards the green pastures and the still waters of a listening ear and a receptive and obedient heart.

CATHERINE MARSHALL

Whether you turn to the right or to the left, your ears will hear a voice behind you, saying, 'This is the way; walk in it.'

ISAIAH 30:21

July 5:
Hard Times

The hard times are not obstacles to the growth of love, although they will constantly seem to be such when we are young. Rather they are a necessary part of the experience by which real love comes to us.

THOMAS H. GREEN

Week Twenty-Seven

July 6:
Time's Arrow

Time goes, you say? Ah, no!
Alas, Time stays, *we* go.

AUSTIN DOBSON

Come what, come may,
time and the hour run through
 the roughest day.

WILLIAM SHAKESPEARE

July 7:
Happy Medium

I gain so much from watching
TV, videos and films, listening
to the radio and reading books.
But I am aware of the dangers
of turning into a mere spectator,
which ought not to be a substitute
for living and contributing in
our own right. There must be
a happy medium, well away from
the extremes of constant activity
and voyeurism.

July 8:
Suddenly

Everyone's voice was suddenly
 lifted;
And beauty came like the setting
 sun:
My heart was shaken with tears;
 and horror
Drifted away...

SIEGFRIED SASSOON

July 9:
Whose Priorities?

Sometimes in life it takes a jolt to get us to take stock of what has been happening.

In hospital I began to consider that in trying to do all those worthy things that everybody wanted me to do, I had become the subject of a tyrannical schedule.

CHARLES COLSON

July 10:
No Chance!

We live in no chance world. All its parts together, and every part separately, are stamped with skill, beauty and purpose.

HENRY DRUMMOND

July 11:
Even to Old Age

Let me grow lovely,
   growing old –
So many fine things do:
Laces and ivory and gold,
And silks need not be new;
And there is healing in old trees,
Old streets a glamour hold;
Why may not I, as well as these,
Grow lovely, growing old?

KARLE WILSON BAKER

July 12:
Smile, Please!

Children certainly brighten up a home. Did you ever see a child under twelve turn off an electric light?

AUTHOR UNKNOWN

Week Twenty-Eight

July 13:
The Best in Me

I love you not only for what you are, but for what I am when I am with you. I love you not only for what you have made of yourself, but for what you are making of me.

AUTHOR UNKNOWN

Is there anyone to whom you could say this? If so, will you?

July 14:
Last Words

Shortly before he was executed by the Nazis, Dietrich Bonhoeffer sent this final message to a friend:

Tell him that for me this is the end but also the beginning.

July 15:
No Dead Letter

I began to write letters to my mother, who had been dead for many years, 'dialoguing' with her on paper about the root causes of my anger. It got a load of anger out of my system without hurting anyone. It was also true dialogue. I began to get insights into my mother's problems and pain, to see things from her angle and to hear her side of the story.

SISTER MARGARET MAGDALEN

Week Twenty-Nine

July 16:
Worry Shared

*Cast all your anxiety on God
because he cares for you.*

1 PETER 5:7

July 17:
Meek but Not Mild

*He guides the humble in what
is right and teaches them his way.*

PSALM 25:9

I wonder what you understand
by 'humble' or 'meek'. Something
I think I have grasped is that
it does not mean mild, mousy,
inferior, doormat-like, mealy-
mouthed, colourless or spineless!
Rather, it is a sign of strength –
a strength that chooses to love,
learn, serve.

July 18:
Were You There?

*Who is my neighbour? He or
she is anyone in need of my care,
concern or company.*

*The bread which you keep belongs
to the hungry; the coat which you
preserve in your wardrobe, to the
naked; the gold which you have
hidden in the ground, to the needy.*

BASIL THE GREAT

July 19:
Taking Stock

*God saw all that he had made,
and it was very good.*

GENESIS 1:31

Week Twenty-Nine

July 20:
What Does it All Mean?

Meaninglessness inhibits fullness of life and is therefore equivalent to illness. Meaning makes a great many things endurable, perhaps everything.

CARL JUNG

If God exists and we are made in his image, we can have real meaning.

FRANCIS SCHAEFFER

July 21:
Break Time

Even beasts of burden must be turned out to grass occasionally; the very sea pauses at ebb and flow; earth keeps the Sabbath of the wintry months; and man must rest or faint.

C.H. SPURGEON

If you don't take breaks, why don't you?

July 22:
Part and Parcel

To be a member is to have neither life, being nor movement, except through the spirit of the body, and for the body.

BLAISE PASCAL

There are many parts, but one body.

1 CORINTHIANS 12:20

To be part of a whole is both humbling and affirming.

Week Thirty

July 23:
Is it True?

*Better a little faith, dearly won,
better launched alone on the infinite
bewilderment of truth, than perish on
the splendid plenty of the richest creeds.*

HENRY DRUMMOND

July 24:
Saying Yes

*Obedience is a particular
means of joy.*

CHARLES WILLIAMS

Blind obedience could lead to
disaster; but choosing the right
master, the right authority, leads
to the kind of obedience that
paradoxically makes for freedom
and joy.

July 25:
Alone or Lonely?

*An enormous technology seems
to have set itself the task of making
it unnecessary for one human being
ever to ask anything of another in the
course of going about his daily business.
We seek more and more privacy, and
feel more and more alienated and
lonely when we get it.*

PHILIP SLATER

July 26:
Valued Qualities

*Whereas American mothers preserve,
often in bronze, their children's first
shoes — celebrating freedom and
independence — a Japanese mother
carefully preserves a small part of her
child's umbilical cord — celebrating
dependence and loyalty.*

STEPHEN FRANKLIN

Week Thirty

July 27:
Connected

We cannot live for ourselves alone. Our lives are connected by a thousand invisible threads, and along these sympathetic fibres our actions run as causes and return to us as results.

HERMAN MELVILLE

July 28:
Clear Enough?

There are two sorts of clarity: the first is bogus clarity in which everything has been oversimplified and difficulties have been ignored; the second is clear enough but not simplistic, and is arrived at only after wrestling with problems and complexities. Anyone who has been through dark times can never settle for superficial clarity.

July 29:
What's the Point?

We strive so hard to get a little further up the ladder, but in the end, what's the point of it all? What good is it really going to do us? Even if the things we worry about do happen, the heavens won't collapse.

WILLIAM BARCLAY

Have you asked yourself recently what you are really striving for?

PETER MARSHALL

Week Thirty-One

July 30:
Friendship at its Best

By friendship you mean the greatest love, the greatest usefulness, the most open communication, the noblest sufferings, the severest truth, the heartiest counsel, and the greatest union of minds of which brave men and women are capable.

JEREMY TAYLOR

I would only want to add that friends can also have the greatest fun together!

July 31:
Be Warned!

The protests of the body are alarm signals.

PAUL TOURNIER

August 1:
Infinite Riches

The present moment holds infinite riches beyond your wildest dreams, but you will only enjoy them to the extent of your faith and love.

JEAN-PIERRE DE CAUSSADE

August 2:
With Hindsight

When I look back over the schedule I kept thirty or forty years ago, I am staggered. Were all those engagements necessary? Every day I was absent from my family is gone for ever.

BILLY GRAHAM

I have heard it said and observed that when people spend their lives trying to please others, they often end up neglecting those they love the most.

Week Thirty-One

August 3:
The Pleasure of Laughter

One should take care not to grow too wise for so great a pleasure of life as laughter.

JOSEPH ADDISON

Small boy to his new baby sister, whom he had been told was a gift from God: 'Quick, before you forget, what does God look like?'

August 4:
True Generosity

True generosity requires more of us than kindly impulse. Above all, it requires imagination — the capacity to see people in all their complexities and needs, and to know how to expend ourselves effectively for them.

I.A.R. WYLIE

August 5:
This Fallen Planet

Things have gone well for me in so many ways, yet there is a part of me that is sick of this fallen planet. I look forward to nothing more than the wonderful brand new morning that is promised. All things will be made new and we shall no longer feel weary or sad, because heaven and earth will be exactly as they were supposed to be.

ADRIAN PLASS

August 6:
Integrity

To thine own self be true,
And it must follow, as the night
the day,
Thou canst not then be false to
any man.

WILLIAM SHAKESPEARE

Being true to ourselves isn't a licence to inflict all our worst characteristics on others! There is no hypocrisy in trying to become the self that we wish we were, as long as we are honest about who and where we actually are for now.

August 7:
Process

Acceptance is nothing but the first step of love. Then it exposes us to a process of growth.

WALTER TROBISCH

August 8:
Touching

There is no organ like the skin. More than that of any other species, our skin is designed not so much for appearance as for relating, for being touched.

PAUL BRAND AND PHILIP YANCEY

August 9:
Love Listens

The first thing genuine love does is to listen deeply, sensitively, receptively to the other person's story and needs. Anyone, like a Job's comforter, who sweeps in to offer the complete explanation or solution is too busy fulfilling his or her own agenda to be truly receptive to others.

Week Thirty-Two

August 10:
Out of Weakness

*My power is made perfect
in weakness.*

2 CORINTHIANS 12:9

Whatever our weakness is, it
can be transformed. If we fail
and prove inadequate in some
situation, we can learn to
understand and empathize with
others in their disappointment
and vulnerability.

August 11:
Life's Gifts

*We must be able to stand back,
refusing to clutch things greedily to
ourselves; yet, at the same time, we
must receive life's gifts with a full
appreciation of their goodness. These
two attitudes do not have to be in
conflict. We need both.*

ANGELA ASHWIN

August 12:
Inside Story

Learning to be really honest
with ourselves is difficult, but
vital if we are ever to experience
growth. Sometimes we prefer
to avoid facing up to something
unpalatable about ourselves or
taking some necessary action.
But all such hedging will get us
nowhere.

Week Thirty-Three

August 13:
Joys to Come

*Weeping may remain for
a night, but rejoicing comes
in the morning.*

PSALM 30:5

*The day must come when joy
prevails and all the makers of misery
are no longer able to infect it.*

C.S. LEWIS

August 14:
Forgive and Forget?

Boy in a letter to his aunt:

*I'm sorry I forgot your birthday.
It would serve me right if you
forgot mine, which is next Friday.*

August 15:
My Favourite Things

These are the things I prize
And gold of dearest worth…
Shadows of clouds that swiftly
pass,
And, after showers,
The smell of flowers
And of the good brown earth —
And best of all, along the way,
Friendship and mirth.

HENRY VAN DYKE

August 16:
The Gift of Sleep

O Sleep! It is a gentle thing,
Beloved from pole to pole.

SAMUEL TAYLOR COLERIDGE

*People who say they sleep like
a baby usually don't have one.*

AUTHOR UNKNOWN

Week Thirty-Three

August 17:
Through the Night

Some of us sleep easily and
well, but some of us don't! For
the latter group of people, there
is a choice: we can lie awake,
or we can do something we enjoy
instead: read, write, make a cuppa,
listen to a tape, watch TV… It
certainly beats clock-watching
and panicking!

August 18:
Metaphors Matter

*As someone has said, 'No man
is an island' packs a punch that's
a hundred times more effective than
saying, 'No one is self-sufficient.'*

If you had to finish the sentence,
'I am…' with a metaphor, what
would it be?

August 19:
Influence

Every soul that touches yours –
Be it the slightest contact –
Gets therefrom some good;
Some little grace; one kindly
    thought;
One aspiration yet unfelt;
One bit of courage
For the darkening sky;
One gleam of faith
To brave the thickening ills of life;
One glimpse of brighter skies –
To make this life worthwhile
And heaven a surer heritage.

GEORGE ELIOT

Week Thirty-Four

August 20:
Invitation to the Weary

Come to me, all you who are
weary and burdened, and I will
give you rest. Take my yoke upon
you and learn from me, for I am
gentle and humble in heart, and
you will find rest for your souls.
For my yoke is easy and my
burden is light.

MATTHEW 11:28–30

August 21:
Love Unlimited

God loves you as though you
are the only person in the world,
and he loves everyone the way
he loves you.

ST AUGUSTINE OF HIPPO

August 22:
Let's Celebrate

I had a friend, now sadly
missed, who could make any
occasion a special celebration.
Do you celebrate friendships,
anniversaries, a sunny day, a new
arrival, an *un*-birthday, finishing
a project…? I guarantee that
on looking back we'd never
regret time spent in these ways.

August 23:
Responses to Change

Do you panic at the thought
of change or, conversely, keep
chopping and changing? Either
way, reflect on the past and the
feelings that lie behind these
responses.

*When you're through changing,
you're through.*

BRUCE BARTON

Week Thirty-Four

August 24:
Understanding

One of the most beautiful qualities
of true friendship is to understand
and to be understood.

SENECA

Friendship is the marriage of the soul.

VOLTAIRE

August 25:
Use and Abuse

Anger at wrong and injustice
is right and should spur us into
action to put things right. But
often the way we get angry is
inappropriate and the wrong
people get the brunt of it.
Being aware of our anger and
its causes or triggers is a good
first step in being in control
of it.

August 26:
Dos and Don'ts

A few extracts from Robert
Fulghum's advice to parents:

Children are not pets;
the life they actually live and the
    life you perceive them to be
    living is not the same life;
don't keep score cards on them;
stay out of their rooms after
    puberty;
don't worry that they never listen
    to you – worry that they are
    watching you;
learn from them;
love them long –
let them go early.

Week Thirty-Five

August 27:
The Glory of a Garden

Although the power of plants can often work instant miracles on distressed souls, the garden has by now firmly lodged itself in our minds as a place where dreams can be fostered and just may come true, where there is always a second chance, a tomorrow.

JANE BROWN

August 28:
Outgoingness

True outgoingness is not about meeting my need to have people with me all the time because I don't like my own company. It's about choosing to be hospitable because I care about you and feel secure enough to offer myself in friendship to you.

August 29:
Cheer Up!

A cheerful heart is good medicine, but a crushed spirit dries up the bones.

PROVERBS 17:22

August 30:
The Joy of Words

I knew then that w-a-t-e-r meant the wonderful cool something that was flowing over my hand. That living word awakened my soul, gave it light, hope, joy, set it free... Everything had a name and each name gave birth to a new thought.

HELEN KELLER

Which words create little explosions of joy inside your head and heart?

August 31:
Getting Sorted

Hard to get down to,
but very satisfying, is a good
clearout every now and again.
There are always things to throw
out or take to the charity shop.
There's always tidying, rearranging,
labelling to do. It's great to end
up with less clutter and a clearer
idea of what you've got and
where it is.

September 1:
Points of View

'Twixt the optimist and the
   pessimist
The difference is droll:
The optimist sees the doughnut
But the pessimist sees the hole.

McLandburgh Wilson

September 2:
The Lord's Prayer

Our Father in heaven,
hallowed be your name,
your kingdom come,
your will be done,
on earth as in heaven.
Give us today our daily bread.
Forgive us our sins
as we forgive those who sin
   against us.
Lead us not into temptation
but deliver us from evil.
For the kingdom, the power,
   and the glory are yours,
now and for ever.
Amen.

The Alternative Service Book 1980

September 3:
Skin

A child put to bed and told that God would be with him, answered, 'I like mummy better – she's got skin.' God chose skin to make himself visible to the world. Now he can be made 'real' through our skin as we reflect something of his character to one another.

September 4:
Off the Treadmill

Turn your back on all high-pressure competitive situations that make climbing the ladder the central focus. Don't let the rat-racing world keep you on its treadmill. Life is more than a climb to the top of the heap.

RICHARD FOSTER

September 5:
Self-Giving Love

Like your landlord becoming your lodger,
like Beethoven queuing up for a ticket to his own concert,
like Picasso painting by numbers,
God lived among us.

SIMON JENKINS

Love is a free giving of oneself for the good of others without demanding a return for ourselves.

September 6:
Sunshine for the Soul

Flowers always make people better, happier and more helpful; they are sunshine, food and medicine to the soul.

LUTHER BURBANK

Week Thirty-Six

September 7:
Life Answers Death

*We are creatures made of dust;
yet we know we were made for
something more. A sense of eternity
resides in our hearts. Living with
this ambivalence is both difficult
and vital. It stretches our souls.*

GERALD L. SITTSER

September 8:
Sublime Living

Lives of great men all remind us
We can make our lives sublime,
And, departing, leave behind us
Footprints on the sands of time.

HENRY WADSWORTH LONGFELLOW

September 9:
The Release of Tears

Men need to be given
permission to experience
the release of tears. Crying
is a human gift and necessity.
Make the most of it!

*When the storms of life are
savage, it is the tree that bends
with the wind that survives.
Tensing up, walling up the heart,
damming up the tears, will
inevitably mean trouble later on,
perhaps years later on.*

CATHERINE MARSHALL

*To bring our deliberately banished
memories back from exile and out
into the open is to recover a sense of
proportion and a basis for hope.*

SISTER MARGARET MAGDALEN

Week Thirty-Seven

September 10:
Service

I do not know what your destiny will be, but one thing I do know — the only ones among you who will really be happy are those who have sought and found how to serve.

ALBERT SCHWEITZER

September 11:
Instrument of Peace

Lord, make me an instrument of your peace.
Where there is hatred let me sow love,
Where there is injury, pardon,
Where there is doubt, faith,
Where there is despair, hope,
Where there is darkness, light,
Where there is sadness, joy.

ST FRANCIS OF ASSISI

September 12:
Praise

Nothing is voiceless in the world:
God hears always
In all created things his echo and his praise.

ANGELUS SILESIUS

September 13:
Less is More

To have what we want is riches, but to be able to do without is power.

GEORGE MACDONALD

September 14:
Blushing

Man is the only animal who blushes — and needs to.

MARK TWAIN

September 15:
Enduring Love

*What a man desires
is unfailing love.*

PROVERBS 19:22

I am sure that what most people want above anything else is one enduring love. Even those of us who are blessed with really good marriages have to face, sooner or later, separation by death. But just to have known faithful, caring, cherishing love for any length of time is a huge blessing and it gives us a little glimpse of the only love that endures for ever and ever.

September 16:
Nothing is Lost

The sweet young Spring has left
   her buds behind;
The memories of Summer, grove
   and stream,
Bright butterflies and birds that
   breast the wind,
Pass like a dream.
Yet faileth not the promise of the
   year;
No waste befalls its savour or its
   scent;
The flowers have fallen, but the
   fruits are here,
Not lost nor spent.

ARTHUR C. DOWNER

Week Thirty-Eight

September 17:
Pain

We all know about the problem of pain, but what about the problem of no pain? People helping leprosy sufferers realized that one of the worst aspects of the disease, resulting in terrible injuries, was that these people had no sense of pain. I am reminded of C.S. Lewis famously commenting that pain was God's megaphone to rouse a deaf world. Some kinds of pain have a purpose.

September 18:
A Grand Adventure

At any moment an unsatisfying life may become once more a grand adventure.

PAUL TOURNIER

September 19:
Aims and Ideals

I live for those who love me,
For those who know me true;
For the heaven that smiles above me,
   me,
And awaits my spirit too;
For the cause that lacks
   assistance,
For the wrong that needs
   resistance,
For the future in the distance,
And the good that I can do.

GEORGE LINNAEUS BANKS

September 20:
A Quiet Tide

Every opening of one's whole self towards some other, every taking upon oneself the burden and the gift of some other, contributes a little to that quiet tide which is flowing back and forth.

JOHN V. TAYLOR

Week Thirty-Eight

September 21:
Paradox

We have the choice of living either with half-truths or with paradox. Living with paradox means accepting two truths that seem incompatible. But how wrong we get things if we don't bank both on love being the most wonderful and the most painful thing in the world; or if we try to detach gifts from responsibilities and freedom from discipline.

September 22:
Love So Amazing

People can only love outside and can only kiss outside, but Mister God can love you right inside, and Mister God can kiss you right inside, so he's different... We are a little bit like Mister God, but not much yet.

FYNN

September 23:
Close to You

The world we live in doesn't make it easy for us to be friends with people and to get close to one another. Relationships involving mutuality, cooperation and interdependence are not exactly encouraged by competitiveness and commercialism. But our desire for closeness and intimacy will not go away. It is part of our human make-up. How can we resist the pressures and draw closer to others?

Week Thirty-Nine

September 24:
Point of Reference

Without a transcendent point of reference, something beyond his identity, man himself shrinks.

DICK KEYES

September 25:
The Wonder of Water

Never in his life had he seen a river before — this sleek, sinuous, full-bodied animal, chasing and chuckling, gripping things with a gurgle and leaving them with a laugh, to fling itself on fresh playmates that shook themselves free, and were caught and held again.

KENNETH GRAHAME

Praised be my Lord for our sister water, who is very serviceable unto us, and humble and precious and clean.

ST FRANCIS OF ASSISI

September 26:
Angels

Whatever you did for one of the least of these brothers of mine, you did for me.

MATTHEW 25:40

In recent years, I have experienced the love and presence of God time and time again through his human 'angels'.

September 27:
A Bit of a Laugh

Low self-esteem support group will meet on Thursday. Please use the back door.

CHURCH NEWS CLIPPING

September 28:
Attitude Matters

Two things reduce prejudice —
education and laughter.

LAURENCE J. PETER

Most men, when they think they
are thinking, are merely rearranging
their prejudices.

KNUTE ROCKNE

September 29:
Grief and Loss

As well as major losses, like
bereavement, life brings smaller
ones. Loss of a place you loved
and lived in; of your children's
childhood; of a job; of a friend
who's moved; of some changing
aspect of yourself… It isn't
weakness to grieve appropriately
for these losses; in fact, it's the
best way to respond to and grow
through them.

September 30:
Contemplation

I do not think I have seen
anything more beautiful than the
bluebell I have been looking at.

GERARD MANLEY HOPKINS

Stretch out by a distinct act of
loving will towards one of the
myriad manifestations of life that
surround you… Pour yourself out
towards it… Deliberate — more,
impassioned — attentiveness is the
condition of success. As to the object
of contemplation, it matters little.
From Alp to insect, anything will do.

EVELYN UNDERHILL

Week Forty

October 1:
Simplify

I keep asking myself: Am I being pressurised to have more than I need? Could I and should I simplify the way I live?

There are two ways to get enough; one is to continue to accumulate more and more. The other is to desire less.

G.K. CHESTERTON

October 2:
Gentle Hands

*O*nly pierced hands
Are gentle enough
To touch some wounds.

ELIZABETH ROONEY

The greatest sense in our body is the touch sense. We feel, we love and hate, are touchy and are touched through the touch corpuscles of our skin.

J. LIONEL TAYLOR

October 3:
True and False Guilt

Without feelings of guilt, humanity is brutalized; without forgiveness and compassion, the consequences can be lethal.

JACK DOMINIAN

Sometimes it is suggested that all guilt is bad, so we should take no notice of it. But to feel bad when we have done wrong or been unkind is to experience *appropriate* guilt. For that, forgiveness is the only healthy, releasing way forward.

Week Forty

October 4:
Realistic Humility

True humility is an authentic
appreciation of ourselves in a way
that neither exaggerates nor
underestimates what we are.

JACK DOMINIAN

October 5:
Paradoxes

Love and truth are another
of those pairs that can seem
incompatible but need to be
held together because they check
and balance each other. We need
to see people both lovingly and
perceptively, with awareness of
their strengths and their
weaknesses.

October 6:
It's True!

The truth will set you free.

JOHN 8:32

'Tis a gift to be simple,
'Tis a gift to be free.

SHAKER HYMN

October 7:
Miracles Everywhere

To me every hour of the light
    and dark is a miracle,
Every cubic inch of space is a
    miracle,
Every square yard of the surface
    of the earth is spread with the
    same,
Every foot of the interior swarms
    with the same.

WALT WHITMAN

Week Forty-One

October 8:
In Good Company

The bad news is: ours is an arduous, long and sometimes tedious journey through Cesspool Cosmos. And observe, it is a walk, not a sprint. The good news is: we are not alone on this demanding pilgrimage, which means that some folks we are travelling with make awfully good models to follow.

CHARLES R. SWINDOLL

October 9:
Time to Reflect

Reflection is a combination of objective and subjective knowing.

DOROTHY ROWE

October 10:
Love and Identity

I tried to write a poem about all the ways in which one's identity is shaped. It became rather a long poem because so many factors are involved: all we inherit and are given; the people we meet and what happens to us; our thoughts, feelings, responses, choices, words and actions. In the last line of the poem I identified the factor that was most important for me. Love. Specifically, my earthly, heavenly loves and friends. My hope is that their love for me and mine for them will more than anything else shape and colour my identity.

Week Forty-One

October 11:
Turning to One Another

Perceptive people all over the world are telling us that we must turn to one another and have real conversations again. This is how change 'from the bottom up' happens — the kind of change that results from people respecting and understanding each other and working together to bring about greater justice and equality.

October 12:
Working at Leisure

When a man's busy, why, leisure
Strikes him as wonderful
    pleasure:
Faith, and at leisure once is he?
Straightway he wants to be busy.

ROBERT BROWNING

October 13:
God So Loved

Dear friends, since God so loved us,
we also ought to love one another.

1 JOHN 4:11

October 14:
May God Hold You

May the road rise up to meet
    you.
May the wind be always at your
    back.
May the sun shine warm upon
    your face,
The rain fall soft upon your
    fields
And until we meet again,
May God hold you in the palm
    of his hand.

CELTIC BLESSING

Week Forty-Two

October 15:
The Road to Knowledge

He that to what he sees, adds observation, and to what he reads, reflection, is in the right road to knowledge, provided that in scrutinizing the hearts of others, he neglects not his own.

CALEB COLTON

October 16:
I Shall Know Why

I shall know why, when time is over,
And I have ceased to wonder why;
I shall forget the drop of anguish
That scalds me now, that scalds me now.

EMILY DICKINSON

October 17:
Acceptance

There are different ways and levels of accepting what happens to us. Someone I know says he is glad he went blind because he has learned and changed so much. I don't think my acceptance of life's hard knocks goes this far! But I absolutely agree with the point that dealing with and bringing good out of trouble and trauma is the only way forward.

October 18:
The Eyes of the Seer

When we know for sure that we are somebodies in God's eyes, we have no need to force other people to make us somebodies.

DEREK COPLEY

Week Forty-Two

October 19:
A New Day

'Tomorrow the adventure begins
anew,' Hodgkins continued.
'Not tomorrow, tonight!' shouted
Moomintroll. And in the foggy dawn
they all tumbled out in the garden.
The eastern sky was a wonderful rose-
petal pink, promising a fine, clear
August day. A new door to the
Unbelievable, the Possible, a new day
that can always bring you anything
if you have no objection to it.

TOVE JANSSON

October 20:
Writing Letters

My father, now in his nineties,
is upset that people don't write
or even reply to letters these days.
Something that helped me greatly
after my husband's sudden death
was writing letters. I called them
Letters to Heaven: some were to
God and some to my husband.
Though extremely painful to
write, I think they helped me
work through a lot of grief
and questions.

October 21:
Meeting Your Needs?

When the satisfaction, security and
development of another person becomes
as significant to you as your own
satisfaction, security and development,
love exists.

HARRY STACK SULLIVAN

Week Forty-Three

October 22:
The Power to Change

Knowledge is often said to be power. But on its own it isn't. We often know what's sensible and best but don't actually do it. Perhaps we don't want it enough, or lack self-discipline or self-belief. Sometimes something as simple as phoning a friend can help to get things moving in the right direction.

October 23:
Taught by Pain

One learns of the pain of others by suffering one's own pain, my father would say, by turning inside oneself, by finding one's own soul. And it is important to know of pain, he said.

CHAIM POTOK

October 24:
Winter Too is Beautiful

There is great beauty in a wintry landscape. Artists know this. Below the surface, in hidden places, growth is happening.

Winter is so beautiful and the wintry portions of my life are those which often give birth to a deeper understanding.

PENNY TRESSLER

October 25:
Faith in God

Two things I have heard about faith which I have found helpful are: first, that it is a reasoning trust; second, that we don't need great faith, but faith in a great God.

Week Forty-Three

October 26:
On Ageing

Teach me the glorious lesson that occasionally it is possible I am mistaken. Keep me reasonably sweet. I do not want to be a saint. Some of them are very hard to live with. But a sour old woman is one of the crowning works of the devil. Help me to extract all possible fun out of life. There are so many funny things around us and I do not want to miss out on any of them.

NUN'S PRAYER

October 27:
Closeness

We have forgotten how close human beings once were to one another.

STUART MILLER

One of the greatest human longings is to be close to someone.

FISHER AND HART

October 28:
Means of Growth

Let me use disappointment as
   material for patience;
Let me use success as
   material for thanksgiving;
Let me use suspense as
   material for perseverance;
Let me use danger as
   material for courage;
Let me use pains as
   material for endurance.

JOHN BAILLIE

Week Forty-Four

October 29:
Two Kinds of Good

There are two kinds of good in human experience: some things are good for something else and some things are simply good in themselves.

RICHARD HOLLOWAY

October 30:
Loving Someone

Loving someone does not simply mean doing things for them; it is much more profound. To love someone is to show them their beauty, their worth and their importance; it is to understand their cries and their body language; it is to rejoice in their presence, spend time in their company and communicate with them. To love is to live a heart-to-heart relationship with another, giving to and receiving from each other.

JEAN VANIER

October 31:
If Only!

In his poem 'The Impercipient', Thomas Hardy describes how alone and left out he feels when everyone else can see 'the glorious distant sea' while he sees nothing but 'a dark and windswept pine'. What's worse, people suggest that his loss of faith is his choice and his fault, and in answer to that, he protests:

O, doth a bird deprived of wings
Go earthbound wilfully?

November 1:
What I Gave I Have

Nothing you have not given away will ever be really yours.

C.S. LEWIS

It is in giving that we receive.

ST FRANCIS OF ASSISI

Week Forty-Four

November 2:
Heart and Soul

*Whatever you do, work at it
with all your heart.*

COLOSSIANS 3:23

November 3:
Rest

*In my Father's house
are many rooms.*

JOHN 14:2

Shall I find comfort, travel-sore
and weak?
Of labour you shall find the sum.
Will there be beds for me and all
who seek?
Yea, beds for all who come.

CHRISTINA ROSSETTI

November 4:
The Best?

*What's the best thing in the
world?
June-rose by May-dew impearled;
Sweet south wind that means no
rain;
Truth, not cruel to a friend;
Pleasure, not in haste to end;
Beauty, not self-decked and curled
Till its pride is over-plain;
Light, that never makes you wink;
Memory that gives no pain;
Love, when, so, you're loved
again.*
What's the best thing in the
world?
– Something out of it, I think.

ELIZABETH BARRETT BROWNING

Week Forty-Five

November 5:
The Process of Becoming

*Identity is found in living
in the midst of a constantly
changing inner and outer world.*

DICK KEYES

November 6:
Good and Clever

If all the good people were
  clever,
And all clever people were good,
The world would be nicer than
  ever
We thought that it possibly
  could.

ELIZABETH WORDSWORTH

November 7:
A Free Captive

I sink in life's alarms
When by myself I stand;
Imprison me within thine arms
And strong shall be my hand.

GEORGE MATHESON

November 8:
Keeping Friends

*The first general rule for friendship
is to be a friend, to be open, natural,
utterly interested; the second rule is
to take time for friendship.*

NELS F.S. FERRÉ

Make new friends but keep the old;
Those are silver, these are gold.

JOSEPH PARRY

Week Forty-Five

November 9:
Nature

How much I have lost by
leaving nature out of my life.

F. SCOTT FITZGERALD

I believe a leaf of grass is not less
than the journey-work of the stars.

WALT WHITMAN

Nature is not a temple but a workshop,
and man's the workman in it.

IVAN TURGENEV

November 10:
Irony

The Royal Society for the Prevention
of Accidents held an exhibition at
Harrogate in 1968. The entire display
fell down.

STEPHEN PILE

November 11:
The Gift of Creation

To live we must daily break the
bread and shed the blood of creation.
When we do this knowingly, lovingly,
skilfully, reverently, it is a sacrament.
When we do it ignorantly, greedily,
clumsily and destructively, it is a
desecration. In such a desecration, we
condemn ourselves to spiritual and
moral loneliness and others to want.

ESTHER DE WAAL

Week Forty-Six

November 12:
A New Dawn

Death is not the end. Death is only putting out the lamp at the rise of a new dawn.

DAVID WATSON

November 13:
Mind Matters

I do not feel obliged to believe that that same God who has endowed us with sense, reason and intellect has intended us to forego their use.

GALILEO GALILEI

The best cosmetic in the world is an active mind that is always finding something new.

MARY MEEK ATKESON

November 14:
What's it All About?

A girl who kept wondering about the meaning of life was told by her parents that such questions were absurd. But one day she suddenly saw with joy that an action could have meaning if it related to some ultimate point of meaning. Another way of putting this might be to say that when our little stories are part of the big one, they can make total sense.

November 15:
Patience is a Virtue!

A hot-tempered man stirs up dissension, but a patient man calms a quarrel. Better a patient man than a warrior, a man who controls his temper than one who takes a city.

PROVERBS 15:18; 16:32

Week Forty-Six

November 16:
Just Imagine!

The imagination has been called the mind's third eye or the mind at play.

As for the sneeze, it climbed to the top of the fir tree and there it lives, Atishoo-ing when the wind blows hard. You can hear it if you listen on a cold winter's night when you are in bed.

ALISON UTTLEY

November 17:
Where the Heart is

Home – a world of strife shut out, a world of love shut in.
Home – a place where the small are great and the great are small.

CHARLES M. CROWE

November 18:
Balanced Living

I read somewhere that a good rule of thumb for any would-be novelist is to think in terms of including action, dialogue and introspection in about equal proportions – about a third each. That way there is pace to keep the story going, conversation to add interest and convey character and introspection – what the characters are thinking and feeling – to add depth.

Good idea for living as well as for writing?

Week Forty-Seven

November 19:
Enthusiasm

O, you gotta get a glory in the
work you do,
A hallelujah chorus in the heart
of you.
Paint, or tell a story, sing, or
shovel coal,
But you gotta get a glory or the
job lacks soul.

AUTHOR UNKNOWN

*Nothing great was ever achieved
without enthusiasm.*

RALPH WALDO EMERSON

November 20:
Searching Far and Wide

*Though we travel the world over
to find the beautiful, we must
carry it with us or we find it not.*

RALPH WALDO EMERSON

November 21:
Music

*After silence, that which comes
nearest to expressing the inexpressible
is music.*

ALDOUS HUXLEY

*I have my own particular sorrows,
loves, delights; and you have yours.
But sorrow, gladness, yearning, hope,
love, belong to us all, in all times
and in all places. Music is the only
means whereby we feel these emotions
in their universality.*

H.A. OVERSTREET

November 22:
Everything but…

*Power can do everything but
the most important thing: it cannot
control love.*

PHILIP YANCEY

Week Forty-Seven

November 23:
Tensions Held

It is a sign of growth when we can hold the tension between knowing and not knowing, belief and doubt, joy and sorrow, having and waiting, love and hate.

MYRA CHAVE-JONES

November 24:
Perspective

When I was a boy of fourteen, my father was so ignorant I could hardly stand to have the man around. But when I got to be twenty-one, I was astonished at how much he had learned in seven years.

MARK TWAIN

November 25:
Pipe Dreams

*W*e are sometimes encouraged by the media to believe we can be anything we really, really want to be. But it's not true, as many people have found to their cost. We need to be real about ourselves and our gifts and make our choices on that basis. And, as has been said many times and in many ways, it is real love that, more than anything else, makes us real.

Week Forty-Eight

November 26:
God Bless

God bless all those that I love,
God bless all those that love me;
God bless all those that love
    those that I love,
And all those that love those
    that love me.

New England Sampler

November 27:
A Blessing

Deep peace of the running wave
    to you,
Deep peace of the flowing air
    to you,
Deep peace of the quiet earth
    to you,
Deep peace of the shining stars
    to you,
Deep peace of the Son of peace
    to you.

Iona Community

November 28:
True Mercy

Where Mercy, Love and Pity
    dwell
There God is dwelling too.

William Blake

November 29:
Picking Up the Pieces

After my bereavement, these
things helped me most. Doing
some of the things that we'd
done together, which gave me
a feeling of continuity. Feeling
purposeful and useful again.
Making the most of my good
memories. Reminding myself
of what I still had — what I *hadn't*
lost. Being aware of the good
coming out of the pain. And,
above all, being loved, cared for,
needed, helped and allowed to be
myself as I was during that time.

Week Forty-Eight

November 30:
An Open Mind

Give me the ability to see good
in unexpected places, and talents
in unexpected people. And give me,
O Lord, the grace to tell them so.

NUN'S PRAYER

Do not forget to entertain strangers,
for by so doing some people have
entertained angels without knowing it.

HEBREWS 13:2

December 1:
Special Places

Give me the clear blue sky over
my head, and the green turf beneath
my feet, a winding road before me,
and a three hours' march to dinner —
and to thinking! I laugh, I run,
I leap, I sing for joy.

WILLIAM HAZLITT

December 2:
Small Mercies

In the aftermath of dreadful
events, I can usually begin to
see little mercies along the lines
of, 'At least, I didn't have to cope
with such and such!' or, 'Thank
goodness for this or that!' And
I think I hear God saying, 'See,
I am still here. I didn't stop that
awful thing happening and I
know you wish I had, but trust
me, I do care…'

Week Forty-Nine

December 3:
Body Beautiful

*What is it, this seamless body
stocking, some two yards square,
this our casing, our facade, that
flushes, pales, perspires, glistens,
glows, furrows, tingles, crawls, itches,
pleasures and pains us all our days,
at once keeper of the organs within,
and sensitive probe, adventurer into
the world outside?*

RICHARD SELZER

*I praise you because I am
fearfully and wonderfully made.*

PSALM 139:14

December 4:
Perfect Peace

*After winter comes summer,
after night the day returns,
after a storm there follows
a great calm.*

ST THOMAS À KEMPIS

December 5:
Simple Delights

*In the aftermath of some
traumatic life events, I now find
that I am very much more aware
of simple delights – everyday,
often taken-for-granted blessings.
Sunrise and sunset. People's
kindnesses. Deliveries to one's
door. Hot and cold water. Wild
flowers, stories, pictures, music...*

December 6:
Ideals

*The ideals which have always
shone before me and filled me with
the joy of living are goodness, beauty
and truth.*

ALBERT EINSTEIN

*I pray thee, O God,
that I may be beautiful within.*

SOCRATES

Week Forty-Nine

December 7:
At Home

No one can be a good host
who is not at home in his own house.

ESTHER DE WAAL

December 8:
Our Inner Kingdom

The unreflected life
is not worth living.

SENECA

It is possible to live with very
little idea of our inside stories.
Listening to ourselves means
reflecting on our life — past
and present; our thoughts and
feelings; moods and attitudes,
hopes and dreams; bodies and
needs. This is not an exercise in
introspection for its own sake;
but a way of growing more whole
and more understanding of others
as well as of ourselves.

December 9:
Courage

Courage is fear that has said
its prayers.

KARLE WILSON BAKER

Courage is resistance to fear,
mastery of fear — not absence of fear.

MARK TWAIN

The hero is no braver than an
ordinary man, but he is brave for
five minutes longer.

RALPH WALDO EMERSON

Week Fifty

December 10:
A World Full of Wonders

If we traced all the body signals involved in walking, we would find in that grinning, perilously balanced toddler a machine of unfathomable complexity.

PAUL BRAND AND PHILIP YANCEY

December 11:
A Revolutionary Prayer

When we pray the Lord's Prayer, we are praying for a personal and social revolution through which the transformation of our world will become a reality.

TONY CAMPOLO

December 12:
Discovering Patterns

As I wrote in my journal, I found that I could discover patterns in my life cycles and seasons.

LUCI SHAW

December 13:
Friend for All Seasons

A friend is a person with whom I may be sincere. Before him, I may think aloud.

RALPH WALDO EMERSON

Give other friends your lighted
   face,
The laughter of the years;
I come to crave a greater grace —
Bring me your tears!

EDWIN MARKHAM

Few delights can equal the mere presence of one whom we trust utterly.

GEORGE MACDONALD

Week Fifty

December 14:
Seeing with the Heart

A truly hospitable – open, receptive – heart is I believe a truly loving one. Not falsely optimistic or falsely humble, and not sentimental, but secure enough to be perceptive and generous; able to see both reality and potential.

The eyes are blind:
one must look with the heart.

ANTOINE DE SAINT-EXUPÉRY

December 15:
Natural Sounds

Every sound is sweet;
Myriads of rivulets hurrying
   through the lawn,
The moan of doves in
   immemorial elms,
And murmuring of innumerable
   bees.

ALFRED, LORD TENNYSON

December 16:
Laughter in Heaven

If you're not allowed to laugh
in heaven, I don't want to go there.

MARTIN LUTHER

I find this reassuring, but it's hard to imagine laughter in a perfect environment. Except the laughter of sheer delight, of course.

Moomintroll burst out laughing.
Not because anything was especially
funny, but just because he felt so
very happy.

TOVE JANSSON

Week Fifty-One

December 17:
Today

Just for today, I will be unafraid.
Especially I will not be afraid to enjoy
what is beautiful and to believe that
as I give to the world, so the world
will give to me.

KENNETH L. HOLMES

December 18:
Commitment and Identity

There is no such thing as a self
waiting to be found. Quite to the
contrary, the self is something waiting
to be created. And there is only one
way to create a self, and that is
through commitment. Only through
commitment do people achieve an
identity and a meaning and a
purpose in life.

TONY CAMPOLO

December 19:
Writing it Down

If you are thinking of keeping
a journal for the coming year,
here are some content ideas.
You might like to keep a list
of 'Angels' (people who come
to your rescue when you need
them); Happy Surprises (happy
events and unexpected blessings);
Unfounded Fears (things you
feared and dreaded that didn't
happen at all or weren't as bad
as you expected them to be);
New Insights and Lessons;
Resolutions and Reflections.

December 20:
Holding on in the Dark

When the darkness comes
I remember truth I discovered
in the light, and I hang on to
that with everything I've got.

STEPHEN BROWN

Week Fifty-One

December 21:
Giving Ourselves Away

Most of us have brief moments when we know with absolute certainty that to give ourselves away in love is the full, perfect satisfaction for which we crave.

H.A. WILLIAMS

December 22:
No Pain, No Gain

O Love! whate'er my lot,
Still let this soul to thee be true –
Rather than have one bliss forgot,
Be all my pains remembered too!

THOMAS MOORE

If you have the capacity for bliss, you have the capacity for pain. The two go together.

December 23:
Best Friends

Don't urge me to leave you or to turn back from you. Where you go I will go, and where you stay I will stay. Your people will be my people and your God my God. Where you die I will die, and there I will be buried.

RUTH 1:16–17

One of the most famous declarations of eternal friendship – and it was from a woman to her mother-in-law!

Week Fifty-Two

December 24:
The Blessing of Giving

*It is more blessed to give
than to receive.*

ACTS 20:35

*Give, and it will be given to you.
A good measure, pressed down,
shaken together and running over,
will be poured into your lap.
For with the measure you use,
it will be measured to you.*

LUKE 6:38

December 25:
Prince of Light

*Peaceful was the night
Wherein the Prince of Light
His reign of peace upon the
earth began.*

JOHN MILTON

December 26:
Outrageous Generosity

*He so loved us that for our sakes
he, through whom time was made,
was made in time. In the manger
he cried like a baby in speechless
infancy — this Word without whom
human eloquence is speechless.*

ST AUGUSTINE OF HIPPO

December 27:
True Love

*Jesus took bread into his hands;
thanked God for it; broke it;
shared it. These four actions of
offering, thanking, breaking and
sharing together show the pattern
of what self-giving love means.*

MICHAEL MAYNE

Week Fifty-Two

December 28:
To God with Love

What can I give him,
Poor as I am?
If I were a shepherd,
I would bring a lamb.
If I were a wise man,
I would do my part.
Yet what I can I give him –
Give my heart.

CHRISTINA ROSSETTI

December 29:
God and Man

The Son of God became the
Son of Man to make the sons of men
the sons of God.

AUTHOR UNKNOWN

He was made what we are that he
might make us what he is himself.

IRENAEUS

December 30:
Light, Peace, Love

Light looked down and beheld
    Darkness.
'Thither will I go,' said Light.
Peace looked down and beheld War.
'Thither will I go,' said Peace.
Love looked down and beheld Hate.
'Thither will I go,' said Love.
So came Light and shone.
So came Peace and gave rest.
So came Love and brought Life.

LAURENCE HOUSMAN

December 31:
Bells

Ring out the old, ring in the new,
Ring happy bells across the snow.
The year is going, let him go;
Ring out the false, ring in the true.

ALFRED, LORD TENNYSON

Thematic Index

Beauty

January 12–14, January 25, January 27, February 8, February 12, February 24–25, March 5, March 7, March 9, March 23, April 11, April 14, April 17, April 19, May 15, May 23, June 1, June 3, June 11, June 14, June 21, July 1, July 8, July 19, September 30, October 7, October 24, November 9, November 20–21, December 1, December 3, December 5–6, December 10, December 15.

Change and Growth

January 1–3, January 5, January 20, March 26, April 13, May 8–9, May 19, July 11, August 7, August 12, August 23, October 1, October 3, October 11, October 28, November 13, November 24, December 31.

Choices and Decisions

February 3, February 17, March 10–11, March 20, March 29, March 31, April 1, April 4, April 15, April 24, April 26, May 11, May 13, May 21, May 24, June 2, June 10, June 25, June 27, July 7, July 24, July 26, August 11, September 1, September 4, September 19–21, October 12, October 22, November 1, November 11, November 15, November 30, December 24.

Thematic Index

Difficult Times

January 28, April 2, May 4, May 25, May 27, May 30, June 18, July 2–5, July 25, August 10, October 16–17, December 2, December 20.

Doubt and Fear

January 23, March 15, May 2, May 14, May 20, May 22, July 23, July 28, August 1, October 6, October 25, October 31, November 7, November 23, December 9, December 17.

Grief and Suffering

January 22, January 24, May 17–18, August 13, September 9, September 17, September 29, October 20, October 23, November 29.

Happiness and Laughter

January 16, January 26, February 4, February 7, February 9–10, April 7, April 12, April 22, April 28, May 5, May 7, May 26, May 28–29, June 7, June 16, June 22–24, June 28, July 12, August 3, August 15, August 22, August 29–30, September 6, September 10, September 12, September 25, September 27, November 10, November 16, December 16, December 22.

Thematic Index

Hope

January 29, February 13, February 18–19, March 2, March 6, March 16, April 5, April 9–10, May 6, June 17, June 29, July 14, August 5, August 27, September 16, September 18, October 8, October 19, November 12, November 19.

Identity and Meaning

January 11, February 11, February 20, February 23, February 27, March 4, March 19, March 22, April 6, April 23, April 30, May 1, May 12, June 4, June 8, July 10, July 20, July 27, July 29, August 6, August 18, September 7–8, September 24, October 4, October 10, October 18, October 27, November 5, November 14, November 25, December 7–8, December 12, December 18, December 29.

Peace and Prayer

January 8, January 19, February 6, February 22, March 1, March 13, March 27, April 16, April 25, May 3, May 10, June 5, June 12, June 20, June 30, July 15–16, August 16–17, August 20, September 2, September 11, October 14, November 3–4, November 26–27, December 4, December 11, December 25.

Thematic Index

Relationships and Love

January 4, January 9–10, January 15, January 18, January 21,
February 5, February 15–16, February 21, February 26, March 14,
March 18, March 24, March 28, April 3, April 8, April 20–21, May 16,
May 31, June 6, June 13, June 19, June 26, July 13, July 17–18, July 22,
July 30, August 4, August 8–9, August 14, August 19, August 21,
August 24, August 28, September 3, September 5, September 15,
September 22–23, September 26, October 2, October 13, October 21,
October 30, November 6, November 8, November 17, November 22,
November 28, December 13–14, December 21, December 23,
December 26–28, December 30.

Time

January 30, March 17, March 21, June 9, July 6, July 9, July 21,
August 2.

Wisdom

January 6–7, January 17, January 31, February 1–2, February 14,
February 28, March 3, March 8, March 12, March 25, April 18,
April 27, April 29, July 31, August 25–26, August 31, September 13–14,
September 28, October 5, October 9, October 15, October 26,
October 29, November 2, November 18, December 19.

Notes:
January

Notes:
February

Notes:
March

Notes:
April

Notes:
May

Notes:
June

Notes:
July

Notes:
August

Notes:
September

Notes:
October

Notes:
November

Notes:
December